For Dad and in memory of Mother—G. I.
For my wife, Jean, and my son, Matthew—T. L.

Special thanks to: Frederick Bland, A.I.A., Partner, Beyer Blinder Belle,
Architects; Cathy Gucfa, Sears Roebuck & Co.; Murphy/Hahn,
Architects; J. S. Porter, Pittsburgh Pane & Glass Co.; Sandra Tomas,
Architectural Draftsman.

Diagram of Tuned Mass Damper originally appeared in Kenneth
Wiesner's article, "Tuned Mass Dampers to Reduce Building Wind
Motion," published by the American Society of Civil Engineers.
Reproduced by permission of the author.

THE BIG BOOK OF REAL
SKYSCRAPERS

By Gina Ingoglia
Associate, American Society of Landscape Architects

Illustrated by Tom LaPadula

Grosset & Dunlap • New York

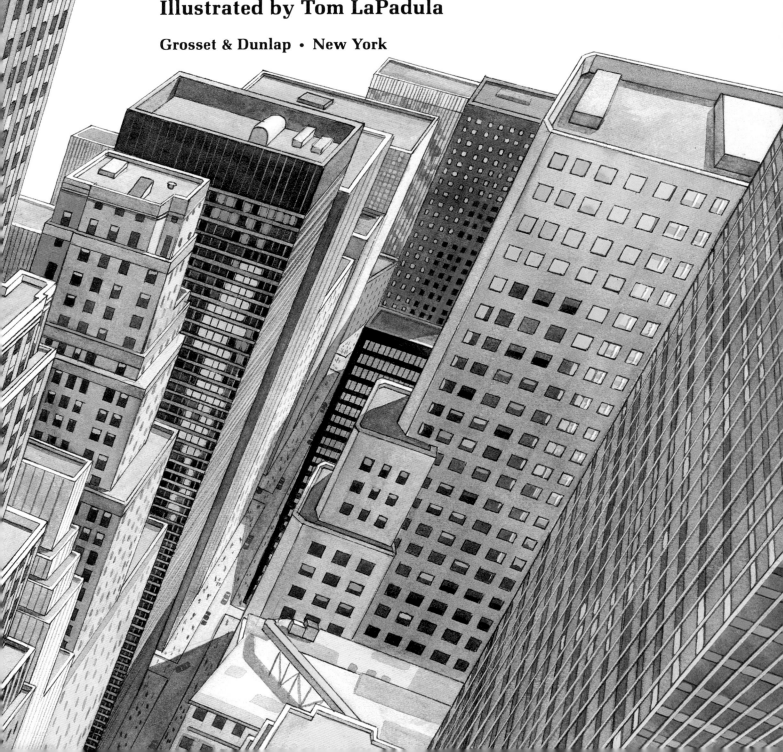

For hundreds of years people all over the world have lived and worked in cities. Whenever more space was needed for new houses or offices, more buildings were constructed and cities continued to spread out over the land.

In the United States during the 1800s, architects (building designers) wished that they could build their cities up instead of out. But there were problems. The taller and heavier a building became, the thicker the walls had to be to hold up the building. Ordinary walls of brick or stone were just too heavy for very tall buildings. People were concerned that they would get much too tired, and it would take too long to climb up and down the many flights of stairs that would be needed.

Despite these obstacles, skillful architects and engineers (construction designers) were finally able to build the first skyscraper. Today, some skyscrapers have over 100 stories, or floors. Thousands of people can work inside a single skyscraper. They can travel from the first floor to the top floor in only seconds! Skyscrapers are sturdy enough to hold up tons of furniture and equipment. Yet the outside walls often look no thicker than many buildings constructed hundreds of years ago.

What happened to make this possible?

Two inventions made the skyscrapers possible. They were the structural steel frame and the elevator.

The Structural Steel Frame

With the invention of structural steel, buildings didn't need to be held up by walls. They could be supported by a steel frame called a superstructure, or skeleton. The walls are attached in sections to the outside of the skeleton. So instead of the walls holding up the building, the building's framework holds up the walls! Because the walls "hang" on the skeleton, they are called curtain walls.

Steel beams bolted together make up the skeleton. It is built on top of a strong base called a foundation. The foundation supports the weight of the building.

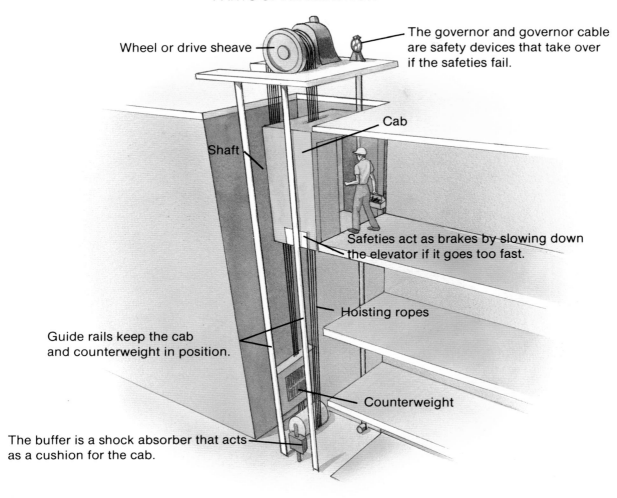

PARTS OF AN ELEVATOR

Wheel or drive sheave

The governor and governor cable are safety devices that take over if the safeties fail.

Cab

Shaft

Safeties act as brakes by slowing down the elevator if it goes too fast.

Hoisting ropes

Guide rails keep the cab and counterweight in position.

Counterweight

The buffer is a shock absorber that acts as a cushion for the cab.

The Elevator

The first passenger elevator was installed in New York City in 1857. The way an elevator works is similar to the way a seesaw works. A seesaw has two riders who act as weights. If the two riders weigh about the same, the two weights are balanced. A seesaw has no motor. The riders push the seesaw up and down with their feet. When one rider goes up, the other rider goes down.

Elevators also have two weights. One weight is the cab with the riders inside. The other weight is called the counterweight. Both weights are attached to hoisting ropes that are pulled over a wheel at the top of the elevator. The elevator is powered by a motor that causes the weights to move. When the cab goes up, the counterweight goes down. When the cab goes down, the counterweight goes up.

Some elevators can travel thirty floors in less time than it takes some people to run up two or three flights of stairs.

The First Skyscraper

Home Insurance Building (completed 1884)
Chicago, Illinois
10 stories
Architect: William LeBaron Jenney

The **Home Insurance Building** is usually referred to as the first skyscraper. The architect, William LeBaron Jenney, started by using an iron framework. When he had finished the first six floors, he heard that steel was being successfully used in the construction of bridges and ships. Jenney decided to try steel on the remainder of his building. He framed the top four floors with steel, and it worked so well that steel skeletons have been used in skyscrapers ever since.

The Home Insurance Building was torn down in 1931.

Where Do Architects Get Ideas?

The **American Surety Building** design is based on the column design, which has been used architecturally for thousands of years. A column is divided into three parts—the capital (top), the shaft (middle), and the base (bottom).

This kind of building design is called tripartite (try-*par*-tight), which means it has three parts.

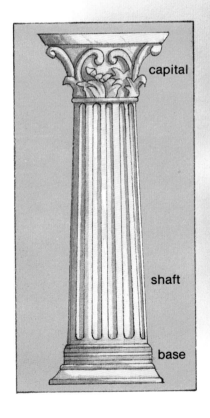

American Surety Building (completed 1894)
New York City
19 stories
Architect: Bruce Price

Venetian campanile

Metropolitan Life Tower (completed 1909)
New York City
50 stories
Architects: Napoleon Le Brun and Sons

The **Metropolitan Life Tower** design comes from a very old clock-tower design called a campanile (cahm-pah-*nee*-lee). The campanile that influenced this skyscraper was built in Venice, Italy, hundreds of years ago. The Metropolitan Life Tower is more than twice as high as the campanile in Venice. The huge clock on the front of the tower is almost three stories tall!

The **Woolworth Building** has a design seen in the beautiful churches built in Europe during the 1100s. The style of architecture is called Gothic (*gah*-thick).

Gothic architecture is delicate-looking even though the buildings are made of heavy stone. The buildings usually have lots of fine detail carved in the outside stone. The spires at the top create a feeling of reaching way up into the sky.

The Woolworth Building was the tallest building in the world for seventeen years.

Sometimes the design of a building is influenced by the land. The **Flatiron Building** was designed to fit on a piece of land shaped like a wedge of pie. The name of the building comes from its shape, which is the same shape as the old-fashioned flatirons that were used at that time to press clothes.

Woolworth Building (completed 1913)
New York City
60 stories
Architect: Cass Gilbert

Gothic tower

Flatiron Building (completed 1903)
New York City
21 stories
Architects: Daniel H. Burnham & Company

flatiron

Chrysler Building (completed 1930)
New York City
77 stories
Architect: William Van Alen

The **Chrysler Building** was built during the exciting years in the mid-to-late 1920s called the Jazz Age. It was a period known for its many new forms of art, music, and architecture. A lot of people think that the Chrysler Building is a symbol of the Jazz Age.

The decorations on the tower were modeled after the hood ornament on 1929 Chrysler automobiles. The tower windows, shaped like triangles, were set between arches of stainless steel.

A 185-foot spire was added on top of the tower because the architect, William Van Alen, wanted his building to be the tallest in the world. The spire was built in secret inside the building. It was put up in one huge 27-ton piece just as the tower was finished. Unfortunately for Van Alen, the Chrysler Building was the tallest building for only a short time. Before it was even finished, work on the much taller Empire State Building had already begun.

Empire State Building Facts

- Tallest building in the world from 1931 to 1970.
- Built in a little over one year.
- Building materials: granite, aluminum, nickel, chrome.
- Steel frame weighs 60,000 tons.
- Elevators travel up to 1,200 feet per minute.
- One and a half million people visit the observation deck every year.
- On a clear day, you can see 80 miles in all directions.
- The top 30 floors are lit in colors for holidays.

In 1945 an Army B-25 bomber crashed into the 79th floor. The pilot and 13 people in the building were killed.

In 1948 hundreds of birds crashed into the tower, confused by the hazy lights seen in the fog. As a result, during migration seasons, lights are turned off on foggy nights.

A 222-foot television antenna was added to the top in 1950.

Empire State Building (completed 1931)
New York City
102 stories
Architects: Shreve, Lamb & Harmon

Skyscraper Designs

Rockefeller Center is one of the most popular places in New York City. For the first time, a group of skyscrapers was built with each one being part of a large architectural design. The tallest building is the 70-story RCA Building.

Rockefeller Center was built on several levels for different uses—from office buildings many stories high, to stores and theaters on the street level, to subways far below the sidewalks.

Rockefeller Center (completed 1932-1940)
New York City
Architects: Benjamin Wistar Morris
Reinhard & Hofmeister
Corbett, Harrison & MacMurray
Hood & Fouilhoux

The large plaza, or open public space, at the street level attracts people all year round. The main entrance to the plaza is lined with benches. Large containers hold attractive plants that are changed according to the season. A lower plaza is an outdoor restaurant when the weather is warm and an ice-skating rink when the weather is cold. Every Christmas a huge evergreen tree is trucked in and trimmed with thousands of lights. During the winter holiday season, Rockefeller Center attracts visitors from all over the world.

Lever House has walls of stainless steel and glass. On sunny days, the blue sky and clouds are mirrored on the shiny curtain walls. Lever House gives people a feeling of light and airiness when they pass by on the street.

The **Seagram Building** has bronze and glass curtain walls that rise straight up behind a plaza, which contains Italian marble benches and two huge fountains. Many people think the Seagram Building is one of the best-designed buildings of the twentieth century. It has perfect details and proportions that are easy to appreciate because the building sits back from the street.

Sears Tower (completed 1974)
Chicago, Illinois
110 stories
Architects: Skidmore, Owings & Merrill

World Trade Center (completed 1976)
New York City
110 stories
Architects: Minoru Yamasaki & Assoc.
          Emery Roth & Sons

The **World Trade Center** has twin towers. Although they have the same number of stories as the Sears Tower, the World Trade Center towers are 104 feet shorter. Each tower is 1,350 feet high. Fifty thousand people work in the World Trade Center and eighty thousand more visit it every day!

Not every elevator in the towers goes to every floor. Express elevators carry people nonstop to certain floors where passengers must switch elevators to travel to the top floors in each tower. The floors where they switch elevators are called sky lobbies.

The **Sears Tower** is the tallest building in the world. It is 1,454 feet high. The unusual structure is a set of square towers connected together. The towers are of different heights and create an almost steplike design. Sears Tower looks like many smaller buildings put together to form one huge skyscraper.

The **megastructure** is a new design in city architecture. Like Rockefeller Center, the megastructure is a group of buildings that forms one architectural design. It too has office space, restaurants, hotels, shops, and plazas. But, unlike Rockefeller Center, these features cannot be seen from the street. The entire megastructure is contained behind a huge wall with no windows and very few entrances—almost like a fort in the city. A megastructure is usually entered by car, and the driver parks inside the structure. Peachtree Plaza is an example of a megastructure.

Peachtree Plaza (completed 1967)
Atlanta, Georgia
Architect: John Portman

Some people like megastructures because the high walls protect them from dangers and speeding traffic on city streets. Others agree that cities have problems, but they think that megastructures, with their high, unfriendly walls, are "turning their backs" on city life. These people think there are better ways than building megastructures to make cities safer places to live and work.

Who's Who?

Many people are involved in planning and constructing a skyscraper. Here are some of them.

The **architect** designs the building. The **landscape architect** designs the roof and the outdoor space around the building.

Surveyors measure the site or location. They make sure the building is placed in exactly the right spot and stays inside the property limits according to the architect's plan.

Engineers go over the architect's plan to see if the design can be constructed safely. They often use computers to decide the best way to construct the skyscraper.

The **cost estimator** determines how much it will cost to build the skyscraper.

The **general contractor** is in charge of the construction. He organizes the workers and keeps track of all supplies and machinery delivered to the site.

Ironworkers, or **boomers**, put up the steel beams for the frame. They are also called **hard hats**. They have a very dangerous job. Ironworkers walk along beams hundreds of feet from the ground without a safety net below!

The **inspector** visits the building to make sure it is being built safely.

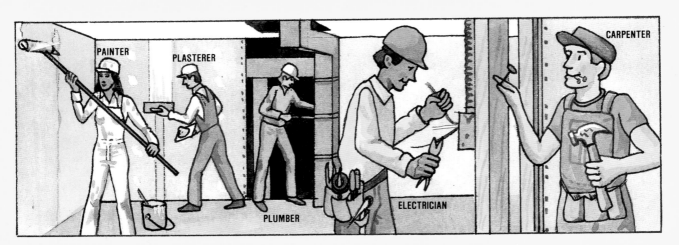

PAINTER   PLASTERER   PLUMBER   ELECTRICIAN   CARPENTER

Finish workers do the interior work on a skyscraper.

Everybody tries to get the skyscraper finished in a short time, but sometimes it takes years to complete.

How Construction Beams Are Made

Construction beams are made of steel. The beams have a special shape that makes them very strong. If you look at their ends, you can see why. These beams are called H beams and I beams.

Each beam is drilled with holes for the bolts. The holes must be in exactly the right spot so the beams can be bolted together by the ironworkers.

Steel is stronger than iron. Iron can be heated so hot that it melts and becomes a liquid. Liquid iron is called molten iron. Steel is formed when molten iron is mixed with limestone and a form of coal called coke.

Iron is found in the ground. It is mined, or dug out, and sent by train to a steel mill.

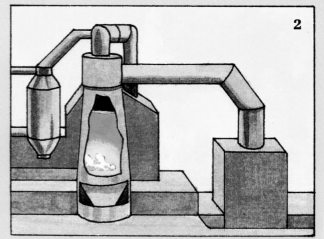

At the mill, the iron, mixed with limestone and coke, is loaded into a huge blast furnace. It is heated into a white-hot liquid. Unwanted waste, called slag, floats to the top and is removed through an opening in the furnace.

The molten iron flows out the bottom into a huge ladle.

A railroad car called a submarine, or hot-metal car, is filled with the molten iron. The submarine carries the molten iron to another furnace that heats and mixes the iron with oxygen. Now the molten iron becomes molten steel.

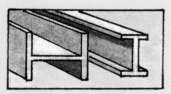

An **H** beam and **I** beam.

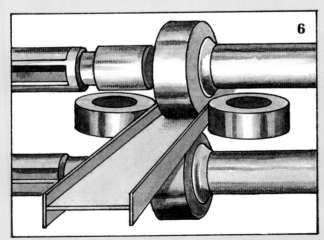

While the ingots are still glowing hot, they are squeezed and rolled into very long H and I beams.

The steel is poured into molds, where it cools enough to become solid on the outside. The mass of molded steel, called an ingot, is still too hot to touch.

When the beams are cool, they are cut with a huge buzz saw. Then holes are drilled into them.

Now the steel beams can be shipped to a city. There they will become part of a brand-new skyscraper.

Choosing the Correct Foundation

The foundation is one of the most important parts of a building. The weight of the whole building rests on it. The type of foundation used depends on the condition of the ground under the building. This ground is called the foundation bed. A hollow tube is drilled into the ground and a sample called a core is brought up and examined to see what kind of ground is under the surface. Then the correct foundation is chosen for the job of holding up the building. Here are some foundations that are used for skyscrapers.

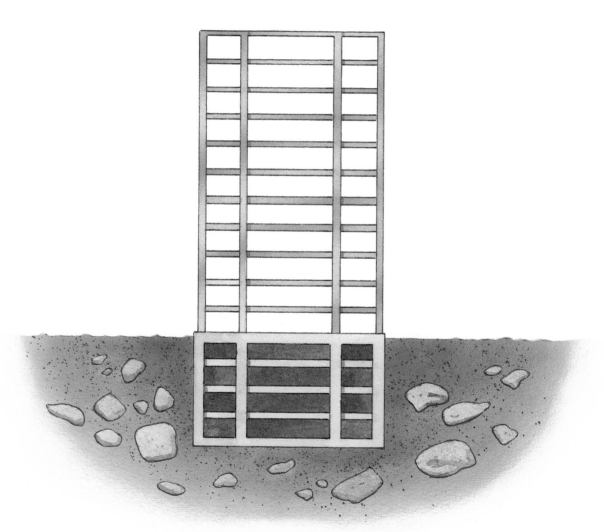

Buoyancy Principle
This foundation involves excavating, or digging out, the bed and removing an amount of earth that weighs exactly the same as the building will weigh when completed. Then the building is erected, or built, in the hole. The part of the building that is underground can be used for parking garages and storage space.

Raft Foundation

For soft beds, where there is no bedrock, a raft foundation is used. The weight of the building is spread out over a raft. It is made of reinforced concrete (concrete with steel rods inside it), or steel mesh (a metallic fencelike material). The raft "floats" on the earth as a raft floats on water.

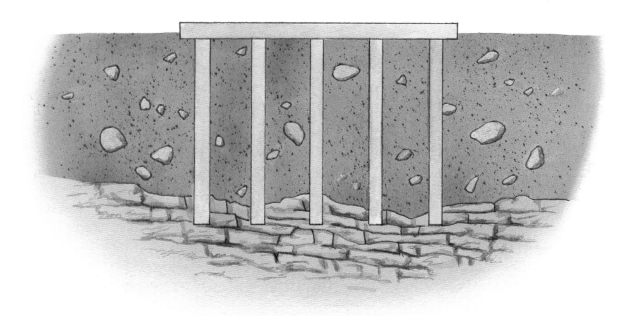

Pile Foundation

If the foundation bed contains bedrock, which is deep-down solid rock, strong columns of steel called piles are driven into the ground. They are pounded into the bedrock by pile drivers.

grader

dynamite mattress

dynamite

Preparing the Construction Site

Before construction begins, the building site is prepared. A wooden fence, often made out of old doors, is put up around the site to protect the public. Peepholes are included for curious "sidewalk superintendents" of all ages.

Sometimes an old building is knocked down by a wrecker's ball or dynamite charges. Dynamite must be handled carefully. After the dynamite sticks are put into the ground, they are covered with a mattress of heavy chain mesh. This will absorb most of the explosion and stop some of the flying dirt, rocks, and bricks. The workers are signaled by whistle blasts—one blast means,

dump truck

front-end loader

backhoe loader

"The dynamite is in place"; two blasts mean, "Take cover"; three blasts mean, "All clear."

Strong machinery clears the site of old bricks, boards, pipes, and other unwanted material. Backhoe loaders dig at one end and scoop at the other. Front-end loaders pick up loads and dump them into waiting dump trucks. The loads are covered to keep them from spilling out. After the site is clear, a grader smooths the ground until it is level.

But the work has only just begun!

Digging the Foundation

concrete mixer

Before digging the hole for the foundation, a deep trench is dug where the building basement will stand. Steel reinforcement bars are wired together and lowered into the trench. Cement is poured down over them. Cement is a powder made out of clay and limestone. After it is mixed with sand, gravel, and water, it hardens and becomes concrete. As the cement mixture in the trench hardens, it forms a concrete wall with the steel reinforcements inside it. Reinforced concrete is extremely strong.

You can't see the wall in the trench because it is under the ground. But as the excavation for the foundation is dug, more and more of the wall is uncovered and becomes visible. The excavation stops at the bottom of the wall. The wall prevents the excavation from caving in. It is also the basement wall for the skyscraper.

Footings, which will support the foundation, now have to be constructed. To make footings for a bedrock foundation, piles are driven into the ground. After they are in place, wooden forms are built around the tops of each pile. Cement is poured into the forms, making the footings.

A steel beam is very heavy, so its weight has to spread evenly over the footing. This is done with a huge block of steel bars called a grillage. The grillage fits between the concrete footing and the beam. The beam will be attached to the grillage with strong anchor bolts.

The foundation is finished. Now it's time for the ironworkers to get busy.

Constructing the Skyscraper

The steel beams are brought by truck to the site. Each beam has been specially marked with white paint so the ironworkers will know where it belongs in the framework.

Putting up the superstructure is like putting together a huge and heavy puzzle. The H beams are called columns. Each one is usually two stories high and can weigh over twenty tons! The I beams are called girders. They are bolted to the sides of the columns, forming the floor beams.

The center part of the building is put up first. It is called the core. Powerful cranes swing the beams into place, where they are bolted together by waiting ironworkers. Instead of working from the street like most cranes, the climbing tower crane rests on the superstructure and is built higher along with the building construction.

Metal sheets called decking are attached to the floor beams. The top is covered with reinforced concrete, making a strong floor. Telephone lines, electric cables, and piping are run through tubes attached to the underside of the decking. Also hanging from the decking, below these lines, cables, and pipes, is the ceiling for the floor below.

While beams are still being added above, curtain wall sections are attached to the finished floor beams. The curtain walls don't support the building. The steel skeleton does that. Curtain walls are just the building's "skin." Sections of them may include windows.

All kinds of activity goes on behind the curtain walls. The finish workers hook up the plumbing, electricity, and telephone lines. The interior walls are put up, painted, and plastered, and the elevators are installed.

Topping-Off Ceremony

It's a great day when the steel skeleton reaches its full height. A celebration called a "topping-off ceremony" is held. The top beam is positioned into place, and an American flag is usually flown from the beam. Sometimes, for good luck, a small evergreen tree is attached.

Everybody involved in the design and construction of the building is invited to the party. The fun doesn't last for long, though. Soon all the workers are back on the job—trying to complete the building on time.

After the building is finished and it becomes a part of the city skyline, each one of the people involved can point to it and say, "See that skyscraper over there? I helped build it!"

Fire Protection

Skyscrapers must be equipped to help prevent fires or to keep them from spreading.

Every steel beam is fireproofed during construction. Steel will not burn, but it is not entirely fireproof. If the beams get extremely hot, they start to melt and become soft and saggy. Fireproofing helps to keep the steel from bending and losing its great strength.

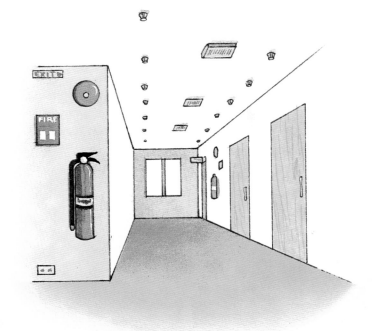

Sprinkler systems, smoke detectors, fire extinguishers, and alarms are put on every floor.

If there is a fire, fireproof stairways give people a safe way to leave the building. The elevators are never used during a fire.

Making Buildings Safe from Wind

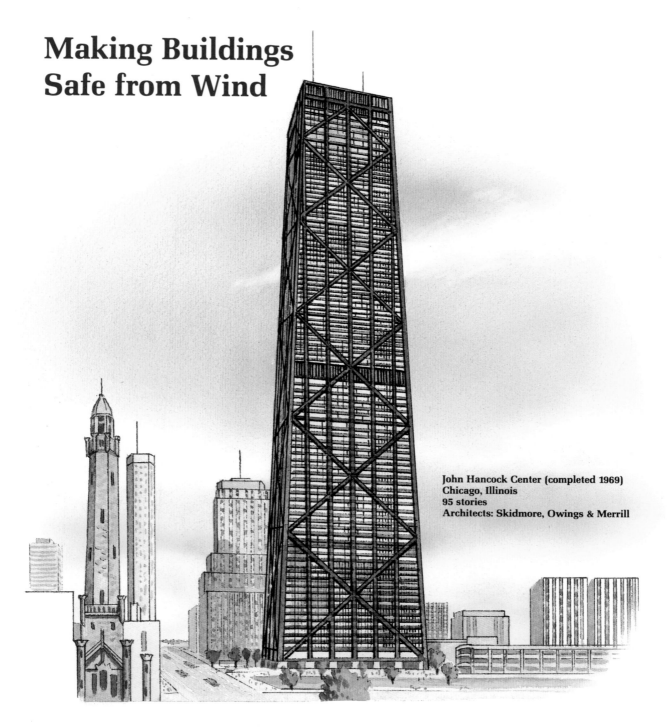

John Hancock Center (completed 1969)
Chicago, Illinois
95 stories
Architects: Skidmore, Owings & Merrill

All tall buildings sway a little in very windy weather. They would sway even more if it weren't for the core that runs down the center of the building. The core is made of reinforced concrete and is the strongest part of the building. It is where the elevators are located. The core's sides are strengthened on every floor with crossed steel beams. This "cross-bracing" adds protection against strong winds.

The **John Hancock Center** is strengthened in an unusual way. The cross-bracing is on the outside of the building and is part of the exterior design.

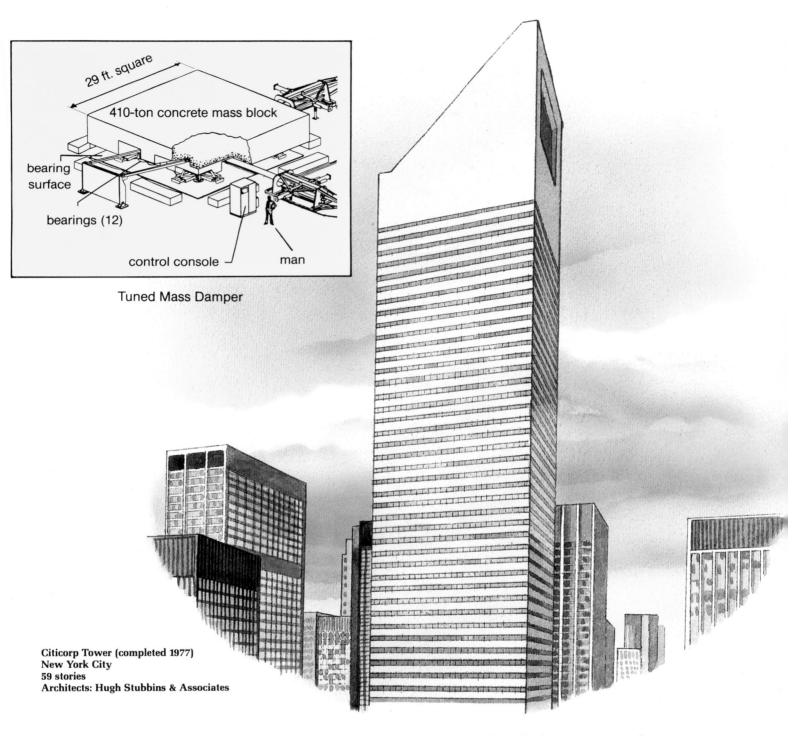

29 ft. square

410-ton concrete mass block

bearing surface

bearings (12)

control console

man

Tuned Mass Damper

Citicorp Tower (completed 1977)
New York City
59 stories
Architects: Hugh Stubbins & Associates

Citicorp Tower, with its sloping roof, is easy to spot in the skyline. But under the sloping roof, a 410-ton block of concrete floats on twelve oil-pressurized bearings, each 22 inches wide and shaped like a hockey puck. The concrete block is called the **tuned mass damper** and is used to lessen the sway of Citicorp Tower. If the building sways more than 1.5 inches per second, a computer sends a signal that causes the block to move. If the wind is pushing the building to the left, the block moves to the right. It balances out the force of the wind. This is called counterbalancing. The damper cuts the sway in half—even in gusty 125-mile-per-hour winds!

Landscape Architecture

A **plaza** is the public outdoor space at the base or bottom of a building. Landscape architects are as careful when designing plazas as architects are when designing buildings. Making use of every inch of space is necessary in the city, especially if it is space where people can sit and walk outdoors. Studies are made of the movement of sunlight and wind in the area. Special attention is paid to the seating design, such as where to use benches, chairs, and tables. A plaza may have water features (fountains or waterfalls), plantings (trees, flowers, or shrubs), and places to eat.

Plazas are places where people can meet and relax. They provide a welcome and refreshing break in the middle of busy city life.

Available outdoor space is not found only at the base of buildings. It may be found also at the top! **Rooftops** are put to good use on many flat-topped skyscrapers.

Some offices provide jogging tracks for their employees to use during their lunch hour. Commuter helicopters, carrying people to and from nearby airports, use rooftop heliports for convenient takeoffs and landings.

Grand rooftop gardens can be designed because the roofs can support a great deal of weight. These "green spaces" often include walks, swimming pools and ponds, trees, and places to sit. Rooftop visitors might easily forget that they are hundreds of feet above traffic tie-ups and crowded city sidewalks.

Skyscrapers Built in the 1980s

Today, some new buildings may look very unusual and modern, but architects still get ideas from old designs.

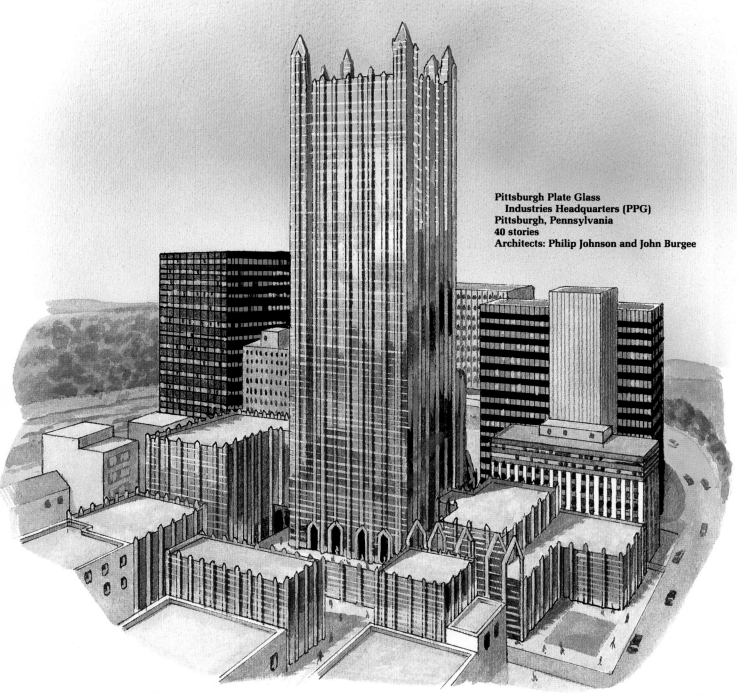

Pittsburgh Plate Glass
  Industries Headquarters (PPG)
Pittsburgh, Pennsylvania
40 stories
Architects: Philip Johnson and John Burgee

The **PPG Building** in Pittsburgh, Pennsylvania, was completed in 1983. Its tower design is based on Gothic architecture just as that of the Woolworth Building was in 1913. But the PPG Building has a glass curtain wall. At night it glows like a glass castle in a fairy tale.

One Liberty Place
Philadelphia, Pennsylvania
61 stories
Architect: Helmut Jahn

American Telephone
and Telegraph Building (AT&T)
New York City
37 stories
Architects: Philip Johnson and John Burgee

The **AT&T Building** was built in New York City in the 1980s. But the top of its tower is similar to Chippendale furniture designs that were used in England during the 1700s.

One Liberty Place in Philadelphia was completed in 1987. Its design was influenced by the Chrysler Building that was built in 1930.

**Hong Kong and Shanghai
Banking Corporation
Hong Kong
45 stories
Architect: Foster Associates**

Bigger and taller skyscrapers are in the planning stages. There are even plans for super skyscrapers reaching over 200 stories high. Some people think skyscrapers are getting too big. Others disagree. They feel that skyscrapers add to the excitement of city life.

Most skyscrapers are located in the United States. But things are changing. Every day skyscrapers are being completed and are creating new city skylines all over the world.

Glossary

aluminum—silver-white lightweight metal

architect—person who designs buildings

bedrock—solid rock found beneath the earth's surface

boomer—nickname for an ironworker who puts up the steel framework for the skyscraper

bronze—yellowish-brown metal made from copper and tin

cement—powder made mostly of clay and limestone

coal—black substance found in the earth that is used for fuel

coke—pure, solid form of coal

column—post that is used for support; another name for H beam

concrete—mixture of cement, sand, gravel, and water; hardens as it dries

core—central and strongest part of a building; houses the elevator shafts

core sample—small collection of rock or earth that is brought to the surface, usually by using a special drill

curtain wall—panels of glass or other materials that hang on the steel skeleton of the skyscraper; forms the outer wall of the building

decking—metal sheets attached to the top of floor beams

dynamite—powerful explosive substance

engineer—person who is concerned with the inner workings and construction of the skyscraper

excavation—hole that is dug to make room for the foundation

fireproofing—spraying or attaching a substance to a surface to protect it from fire; also, the substance used for this

footing—part of the foundation to which the base of the steel structure is attached

foundation—the strong base for a building

girder—another name for I beam

grillage—huge framework of steel bars used for spreading the weight of the structure over the footing

H beam—long column that is part of the steel framework

hard hat—protective hat made of plastic or aluminum; also, a nickname for a worker who puts up steel beams on a skyscraper

heliport—landing and takeoff place for a helicopter

I beam—beam that is bolted to the side of the H beam, forming the floor

ingot—mass of molded steel

iron—brownish ore found in the earth

ironworker—person who drills and shapes the steel; also, person (hard hat) who puts up steel beams

landscape architect—person who designs the land around buildings, including plazas and rooftops

ladle—very deep spoonlike container that is used to pour molten steel

limestone—rock that is formed underwater, over millions of years, usually from shells on the bottom of the sea

mined—removed from the earth

molten—glowing, heated into a liquid

nickel—hard silver-white metal that can be highly polished

ore—naturally formed substance found in the earth, which can be mined and used by people

plaza—open public place in a city or town

pile—strong column of steel that is driven into bedrock as part of the foundation

reinforced concrete—concrete that is strengthened with steel bars inside

site—area where the building stands

skeleton—steel framework of a skyscraper

skin—another name for curtain wall

skyline—outline of buildings against the sky

skyscraper—very tall building that has a steel frame, an inner core, and an elevator

spire—long, narrow tip or point on top of a building

stainless steel—steel that resists rust or stain

steelworker—person who works in the steel mill, changing iron into steel

stories—another word used to describe the height of a building; the number of floors

tower—tall upper section of a building

trench—narrow, long, deep hole

tripartite—having three parts

The Tallest Buildings in the World Past and Present

Year Completed	Building	Height
1974	Sears Tower, Chicago, Illinois	1,454 feet
1976	World Trade Center, New York City	1,350 feet
1931	Empire State Building, New York City	1,250 feet
1930	Chrysler Building, New York City	1,046 feet
1929	Chase Manhattan Bank, New York City	927 feet
1913	Woolworth Building, New York City	792 feet
1909	Metropolitan Life Tower, New York City	700 feet
1908	Singer Building, New York City	612 feet
1899	Park Row Building, New York City	383 feet
1894	American Surety Building, New York City	312 feet
1890	New York World Building, New York City	309 feet
1846	Trinity Church spire, New York City	284 feet